96 – AND ALL THAT!
A Collection of Poems

by

LLOYD KEMP

ISBN: 978-1-905795-74-1
Published by Aspect Design
and printed and bound at their premises
89 Newtown Road, Malvern, WR14 1PD

Acknowledgements

I am indebted to my friend Dorothy for
the cover photograph, which began life as a
snapshot taken during a visit from Australia
with her husband Bruce, to whom I am equally
indebted for many discussions concerning the
lay-out and content of this book. Likewise, I am
deeply grateful to my friends Barry and Maureen, for
their continued help and encouragement at all times.

It will be seen from the list of Contents which follows, that the poems have been assembled in the alphabetical order of their titles. At first sight this may seem to be rather arbitrary. However, as the reader's acquaintance with the poems grows, it will be realized that their subject matter is wide-ranging – from the light-hearted and distinctly quirky, to those concerned with some of the deepest aspects of this human life of ours.

So, often, the next poem will come as something of a surprise. And that's how I like it! – after all, Life itself is *full* of surprises, isn't it?

Contents

PROLOGUE

96 – And All That!

Yes!
In just a year
I've moved on –
from a denary
ninety-five, to a
duodecimal
eight dozen; and –
going one better –
next year's classified
a "prime".

And, after that,
comes a humble
ninety-eight,
with nothing more
as a claim to fame
than being
divisible by
two and seven.
But wait! –
it's followed, then,
by one divisible
by *nine,* and, yes,
eleven, which
must surely
cast a shadow
over what would
otherwise have been
plain ninety-nine.

Yet!
that said,
it is (when all's
said and done)
just one short
of a century –
the cherished
goal of any
self-respecting
batsman.

So – 'Go for it!',
did I hear you say?
'Swing that bat, and
get a four –
at ninety-six,
you need no more –
it'll take you straight
to your hundred,
and a letter from
the Queen!'

Sorry! That boundary
I hit was just a
flight of fancy:

it's back to Earth now –
and life at a modest
ninety-six.

----------- A Make-over For Your Day -----------

Getting up can be like
the rising of the Sun:
the start of a new-born
day, and not merely
yesterday, ongoing,
with sunrise taking up
where the setting sun
left off.

So – begin at the
very beginning,
and give first thought
to that body of yours,
as, reluctantly, it
forsakes the
womb of
bed:

chemically, a mere
assemblage of
lifeless elements,
selected, pre-natally,
from an available
ninety-four, but
given life – yes! –
life!

Then, as your feet touch
the bedroom floor, spend a
quality moment or two,
thinking, 'Just what do we
mean by *"life"*?'

What's that?
You don't know?
Not to worry! –
no-one else
does, either.

So, your day
can indeed begin –
*un-*like any other –
with a sense of *wonder* :
and what a pre-breakfast
tonic *that* can be!
Just *think,* "The gift of
another whole day,
of the *miracle*
we call *"life"!* '

And, then, the day long,
think *"miracle"* over and
again; and you'll find there's been
at least one more,
which affects the very
colours you see:

fact is,
there's no sign of
blues among the
whole gamut of
spectral hues
that make up
the light that
now illumines
your day, re-born.

13

---------- **A Matter of Survival** -----------

'Live, and let live' –
a difficult pill to swallow
when ants are running wild
on the work-top in your kitchen;
yet, declaring war on them
no easy option either,
clinging to their lives
as determinedly as I
to mine: I, with my
balanced diet, and
daily quota of vitamins,
anti-oxidants, proteins,
and the like, and they
with nothing but
six legs to save them
from an untimely end –
as they scuttle off at
their equivalent of
sixty miles an hour;
a steel-hard shell as well,
making a second –
even a third blow
necessary to
send them to
their end.

A few hours of all-out
war left the worktop a sad,
empty, and accusing space,
devoid of the life that
had flourished there,
so little time before.

A pyrrhic victory
I deemed it then –
over creatures who had
sought nothing more than
their daily sustenance:
a taste of honey
from a single drop,
loose on the bench,
or a brief nibble
at a solitary crumb:
surely, little enough
to ask of life?

But – be that as it may:
they were, for me, in the
wrong place, and at the
wrong time, too.

And I, alas,
for them.

A Touch of Tinnitus

producing, deep
within my ear,
the sound of
a single note,
rising, then
falling a whole
octave, over and
again, in step with
my beating heart.

So why did such
oddity seem
so familiar –
as well, strike a
warning note?
Ah – was my heart's
telephone
off the hook?
And – if so –
how many calls
on my love had
come and gone
unheeded?

----------- All Change For The Future ------------

'It can't *possibly* be
as bad as they say.
I mean, I'd have to
change the whole
of my day – leave the
car at home, and
walk quite a way to
catch a bus to work:
It *can't* be
as bad as
that.

'What's more –
it'd spell the end of
all those goodies flown in
from abroad. You know:
fresh mangoes from
India, pineapples
from Paraguay, and
apples and oranges
all the year round, from
who knows where.

'*And* – to cap it all –
it'd mean staying
in England for our
holidays. Just
think of *that!* –
I mean to say – life
just wouldn't be
worth *living.*

'What's that you say:
we're living on
borrowed time? How
stupid can you get!
Time's *time: our* time's
our *own,* to live as
we think fit – as
those did, who've gone
before, and those
who'll come after.

'Come again? – those
who've gone before
didn't borrow any time
from us, and *that's*
why we've been free
to live as we have? –
and even borrow time
from those to come?
You've certainly got
your work cut out
to convince me
of all *that!*

'Did I hear aright? –
if I go on like this,
events will relieve you
of the need? *Huh* –
we'll see about *that!*'

'You're right.
We shall.'

As Usual...?

There was nothing
unusual about the way
my day had begun,
sitting, as I was,
in my favourite chair,
my gaze fixed,
contemplatively,
on the horizon:
a past master at
being its usual self,
day on day.

But – just then – and
as from nowhere,
there flashed before my
inner eye a vision
of a veritable host
of – no – *not* angels:
'down to earth'
as they were,
in so many ways;
but heavenly beings,
nonetheless – albeit
workaday.

And their task
(I understood)
was to help us
humans over the
stile we so often
have to climb,
to gain access
to our day: yes! –
a *host* of them
hurrying and
scurrying
back and forth,
simply on
my behalf!

And my day?
How *could* it be
'as usual',
after that?

At Home...

They have no tongues,
and yet speak volumes,
no minds to call their own,
yet storing memories that
can span centuries – even
millennia; their hearts
stone-hard, yet
warming ours.

> The more time spent
> in their company, the more
> we understand – and come to
> love – their idiosyncrasies,
> especially those pertaining
> to old age; their beauty
> timeless, and beyond our
> apprehension – the bonds
> forged by long association
> with even the humblest,
> among the strongest
> forged by Man;

the meanest mere
mud walls and grass
roofs – yet spelling
home for those who
live and die within
their lowly confines;
the noblest – with their
fan-vaulting, and
heavenward-pointing
spires (or golden, sun-
rivalling domes) – built by
Man the Architect, in praise
of his Creator: each and all,
from the meanest to the
noblest, a holy place,
a living space, where we
can be at home to God –
or God at home to us.

---------- Bereavement ----------

Many said
that it was over now;
others, that I should be thankful;
a few (I fear) that it was simply
God's will that had been done,
(like the hurricane last year) –
but *I* knew the life, which,
in my heart,
had only just begun.

Death gave it birth: your passing
the cosmic contraction
that propelled me
on the head-first journey
through the tortuous tunnel
of fierce disbelief,
with pain beyond thought,
into a future
furnished
with an empty chair,
an empty bed,
coats still hanging, ready,
in the hall;
your place at table vacant,
meal on meal.

Morning upon morning,
listless and leaden-eyed
I lie,
hoping the world
will pass me by.
What chance of that? –
the harsh light of reality
leaves no margin
for the re-interpretation
of events;
better to weep my way
into the crevices
of yet another day –
others, perchance,
will neither find
nor even seek me
there.

But –
tread warily;
at every twist and turn
of time
and space
there lies in wait
some devastating evocation
of the past,
beyond tears –
from a paper scrap,
with frail words
traced by that rebellious hand,
to your first calliper, lurking
in the dark depths
of a wardrobe
where I sought
a long-lost pair of shoes.
(God alone knows
the volumes spoken
by a piece of bent iron
fitted with a leather thong
and metal peg –
the vision, too,
that it evoked
of you,
with your strapped leg
and walking frame,
and those first faltering steps –
God, indeed, alone knows
the courage that you showed.)

Beyond tears, yes,
but weep, noneless;
grief's work
will not be done,
till grief itself
dies, in childbirth –
its progeny hope's glimmer,
lighting the darkest recess
of my breaking heart.

(1988)

Body Language

It had been unkind to me
(or so it seemed), and I
deemed it at best a
nuisance, and at worst
a veritable enemy.

That is, until, one day,
quite suddenly, it seemed
to say to me that,
far from deserving ·
of my animosity,
it *needed* me to
befriend it: yes −
befriend it!

It wasn't easy:
it went against the grain;
but how things have changed,
since I responded to its
cri de coeur! −

we get along so much
better now, I and my
stiff back.

Body Matters

We wouldn't sit cross-legged
before the Queen, nor
her natural dignity demean,
with folded arms, or
other casual posture.

How was it then? – that,
in the stillness of
first light, as I sought to
become aware of the
presence of none other
than God - yes - His very
Self, I found that I was
sitting, legs crossed,
an elbow on the arm
of my favourite
easy chair.

I closed my book,
uncrossed my legs,
and arranged myself
four-square in my
chair, arms limp, and
palms up-turned,
receptively – to learn,
afresh, that as we wait
on God, it needs to be
not only with our
hearts and minds,
but with our
bodies,
too.

Computers? – UGH!

For two long hours
I'd laboured, searching
for words that would match
the depth of my concern –
nothing less than the threat
to the future of civilization
(it was an email to my MP...).

My finger was poised,
ready to click on 'Send',
when caution sounded
a warning note:
'Sleep on it,' it said,
'You may want to change
the odd word or two –
you need to get it right.'
So I opted for
'Move to folder', and
'Drafts', for overnight.

It was then
that the computer –
in a neat little box,
the likes of which
I'd never seen before –
flagged up the words
'Cannot save the message,
an error has occurred.
OK?'

Not to worry! We'll
soon get round all *that!* –
'Copy', then 'Paste' into
a brand-new folder, and
'Save' it there! So I
promptly clicked 'OK'.

Imagine, then, my horror,
when hundreds of hard-wrought
words disappeared completely –
never to be seen again.

Little had I realized
that the computer –
in the role of a
hot-gospelling
evangelist – had been
telling me that my text
was beyond redemption –
that it just could *not* be
saved, and would be
committed,
there and then, to –
well – you know where.

Could It Be?

Early morning
gives no warning
of a sunset
less than eternity away:
no need to plan the day.

Mid-morning
is refreshment time –
let's take a breather
from our play
(the sunshine has surely
come to stay).

High noon,
and native powers
intoxicate
with the sense
that the choice is ours:
there is *nothing*
we could not do
if we wanted to –
but we don't.

By afternoon
the shadow
of a doubt
appears:
the sun seems
not quite so high
(could it be
that it threatens
to set – and that
in a finite time?).

Late afternoon,
and a nip in the air –
better to have a care –
there is no doubt now
that the night exists,
and the light is getting low.

But – could it be
that sun's dying glow
yet symbols
a promise, born of
diminishment,
and fulfilled
at day's end?

Curl Up Cosily

Pull up the chairs!
Poke up the fire!
And curl up cosily! —
for this week's
Colour Supplement
invites us
to choose
where we might go
to escape
the winter
within.

    And let the chatter
    be loud enough
    that the sound
    of the moan
    in the wind
    may be drowned.

Turn on the light!
Draw curtains tight!
(Yes! turn on
sweet music, too),
and we'll play a game
of make-believe —
that there *is* no darkness
outside:
better to bask in
fluorescent tube's light
than risk
an encounter
with God,
in the night.

Edges and Ledges

I had clambered
(as best I could)
onto a ledge
so narrow that
I felt dangerously
close to either edge;
no finger or foot holds –
nothing (it seemed) to
prevent me from a fall
from which I could
easily have woken up
in hospital, or even my
final resting place.

Suddenly, then, and
apprehension had turned
to sheer panic, as I
felt an almighty tug
on one of my legs,
capable of
removing me
altogether from
my perilous perch,
and sending me
hurtling down to
Mother Earth.
'Stop!' I shouted,
'I'm falling off.'
'You know I'd never
have let that happen,'
he murmured,
reassuringly.

But it didn't end there:
his fingers were probing
my back again.
'It's free!', he said,
excitedly. And – it's true –
I got down from that
lofty ledge much easier
than I'd clambered onto it;

you're right –
it was an
osteopathic
couch.

Evolution Revisited

Failing to get
even a mention in
"The Origin of Species",
it has remained
undocumented
ever since: to wit –
that the human heart
had developed
eyes and ears
of its own –
enabling
us humans
to look and listen
with our hearts,
and not simply with
our logic-laden
heads.

First Things First!

Everything stops
for a poem.

What *was* it
that I was about
to do? Ah, yes —
wash, shave, then
dress, and have
my breakfast.

But the world won't
come to an end
if my facial hair grows
infinitesimally
longer, or even if,
for another hour
or so, my face
should go unwashed.
And there's no-one —
but *no*-one! — to
see me in my
underwear, *or*
hear my stomach
rumble.

No! The *world*
won't come to
an end, but —
should I to such
trivial matters
as washing,
shaving, and
eating, first
attend —
my *poem*
might.

Full Circle

The very quest
for meaning
in our lives
is – in itself –
meaning-full.

------------ **Games You're Not Likely to Win** ------------

You'd never believe it,
but my cleaning lady
plays games with me.
It's her idea, not mine,
and the game she enjoys
the most was called
"Hunt the Thimble"
when I was a lad;
but she's changed the
name, and – indeed –
the game: it's now called
"Hunt Whatever" –
which means "whatever
she chooses on the day" –
from a gnarled old knife
that's seen better days
(but none the less
a favourite), to a
precious hoard of
'this and that', which,
long since, you've
convinced yourself
you couldn't *possibly*
do without.

Her genius lies in
spurning all the places
where you would think
to look, in favour of
the most *unlikely* place
of all: once there, it'd
take a year and a day
to find it. You're right! –
it's a game you're
never likely
to win.

Impatient, if not irate
by now, in desperation
you ring her. But she promptly
turns the call itself into
yet *another* game: this time
called "Passing the Buck",
the object quite simple:
to convince you that, if
what*ever* it is, is
wherever it is,
it *must* have been *you*
who put it there...

And her trump card? –
to wear, throughout,
a certain air of
damaged pride:
that you should
ever have thought
a cleaning lady
could be anything but
'squeaky clean'.

You see what I mean?

Holy Riddle

To be
un-answered,
is sometimes
the *answer*
to our prayer.

Holy Spree

I woke, momentarily,
from a nightmare that
had more than matched
the harsh reality of
the day, scarce past.
Turning over
in my bed, I must,
as well, have turned over
whole chapters in
The Book of Dreams –
skipping from the earliest,
'Classic Nightmares', to the
very last, on 'The Joys of
Simply Being Alive':
when sleep resumed,
gambolling, foot-free
as a fairy, across
a countryside
that could but be
the stuff of dreams –
sliding down grassy
banks, leaping over
tumbling streams, and
swinging from branch
to branch of low-
growing trees, the
music of laughter
the backdrop
to the day.

Was it
merely I that
had turned over? –
or had my life
turned a new leaf
too, poised to start
a new chapter,
not merely in the
Book of Dreams,
but the Book of Life,
as well?
And foreshadowed
in a dream.

----------- **"It's An Ill Wind..."** -----------

Confronted by it,
whenever I sought to
rest my weary eyes
on the view from my
sitting-room window,
I have to admit that
(unsparing in my
choice of adjectives)
I *did* call it
'that inescapable
telephone pole: a black
stripe – a vicious swipe
from top to bottom of
the view, severing the
skyline, and ripping through
the patchwork of corn-yellow,
and cattle-grazing green,
to bulldoze its way
down through the valley
that lies between…. that
brutally obtrusive, all-
pervasive, creosoted
wooden pole.'

Yes – there it was, and
there it would remain:
who, or what, could remove
such a 'black, vicious swipe'
which was doing its best to
cancel out the landscape? –
it would take the biceps
of a mythological
giant, even to
attempt it.

But inescapable?
Came the day –
or rather, the night –
that was to prove me
wrong. For, at first light,
when I drew the curtains,
there it was – *gone!* Well –
not quite; but keeling over
dangerously, and plainly
in its death throes;
struck down, not by
a hypothetical giant,
but a rampant
lorry.

The undertakers,
soon on the scene,
were quick to remove
the body. And –
full three weeks on –
here am I,
enjoying the view,
unsullied still –
courtesy
black ice.

Life – a Voyage

I had quit
the haven of sleep,
and was out on the
sea of life again,
my tiny barque
motionless – mirrored
in the surface of the
calmest of calm seas –
its canvas flat
against the mast,
awaiting the
motivating
breeze.

There wasn't long to
wait, and soon I was
about the business of
navigating my way
across life's ocean,
for another day;

and then,
nightfall again –
my barque hove to,
in a place of quiet,
not far from sleep,
where, shortly, I
would once more be
dropping anchor
for the night.

**Love —
and the
Selfish Gene**

I should tell you
that when I look
at my daughter,
it is not with the
self-satisfaction
of knowing that
she is a conveyor
of my genes:

it has nothing at all
to do with Self,
and everything
to do with
the Other.

It is love.

Mirabile Dictu

Many there are who
all but worship him,
lying prostrate,
and near-naked,
in his presence –
despite the risk
to life and limb.

But, should his
scorching looks
perchance be
turned my way,
they are, as if
by magic, changed:
death-dealing rays
to life-giving words,
heart-halting beams to
soul-stirring music
of the spheres
(it could well be a
Beethoven symphony);
this seeming miracle
wrought, on my behalf –
yes! – by a radio,
solar-powered.

New Year: Best Intentions, or "Please-Don't-Mentions"?

How can we rest? – we who
have just exchanged the warmth
of a bedroom for the even greater
warmth of bed; yet, as we did so,
were there many, spreading a
single thread-bare blanket
over a frozen pavement,
for *their* bed.

How can we rest? – we who
have a 'night-cap' in our stomachs
lulling us to sleep, when there are
those – by the billion – kept awake
by the emptiness
of theirs.

How can we rest? – we who
just bade "Goodnight" to a
loving spouse – whilst, night on night,
there are those who, already
leading loveless lives, are treated
as merely 'in the way', and
ordered to move on:
'Out of sight, out of mind,'
as you might say.

Yes, indeed, how *can* we rest,
till each and all of these, our
fellow humans, enjoy, with us,
the God-given blessings of
fair-sharing Mother Earth?

Not Pots of Money,
but
Pots of Song

Some weeks ago,
a blackbird set up home
in my cypress tree,
and – guess what! - he's
stolen a march on the
traffic, streaming by.

You see,
it was all down to
the double-glazing
I'd recently installed,
which had, incidentally,
quelled the traffic's roar,
and (I feared) would, likewise,
banish from my sitting-room
the blackbird's heaven-sent song.
Or so I thought.

Imagine, then, my
disbelief, when – as I
watched the traffic
silently speeding past –
my blackbird started
to *sing* to me as if
he were there,
in the room with me.
How *could* he have
worked such magic?

A quick trip to the garden,
to find that it was yet
another case of "Simple,
my dear Watson!":
perched, as he was,
on the chimney pot –
with the *flue* his
private line
to me!

And I wondered:
was knowledge of
the facilities
offered to blackbirds
by chimney pots
written on their
genes?

Objets D'Art?

They were dumped
on the counter of a
market stall:

"Two Pounds each,"
the notice said,
"and every one
with a baby inside."

Startled,
I looked again,
to find myself
confronted by a
heap – yes –
a *heap* of what I
adjudged to be
objets d'art, and
pregnant ones at that.

What matter that they'd
stretched a point
with the ducks and frogs? –
they'd got it right
with the elephants
and camels: each
with a tiny one inside!
How did they *do* it? –
and at Two Pounds apiece.
Eastern
craftsmanship –
and Western
exploitation?

Occam's Razor:
A Poem for Easter

If – as many
have contended –
their intention had been
to deceive, then it was
hardly the best way
to set about their
task: to admit that
one of them had
mistaken him, yes,
mistaken him
for the *gardener!* –
that is, until he
spoke her name
in that *un*-mistakable
voice of his. Nor did it
help, to say that they
didn't believe her –
scurrying off, to
see for themselves.

Ordinary folk that they
were, one would think they
would simply have said,
"The body *wasn't there*" –
full stop. But, fact was,
that in the instant, their
attention had been drawn
to seeming trivialities,
shrouded, nonetheless,
in a mystery for which
they could find but
faltering words to
describe what had
riveted their
attention.

Even so, many there are,
who believe that the napkin –
baldly described as being
"wrapped together and in a
place by itself" – had been
neatly folded, and put
to one side, by the
risen Christ
himself;

whilst others would have it
that what those words implied –
halting though they be –
was nothing less than that

the cloth wrapped round the
body, and the napkin round
the head, had, in fact, stayed
undisturbed: the body had
simply *escaped* from them.

And – to bring us
right up to the minute
(it was found on the Internet) –
a piece, so it's said, of
ancient Jewish folk lore:
that a *folded*, rather than
screwed-up napkin, left
on the table by the
master of the house,
meant that he hadn't
finished – and
would soon be
coming back.

Be *all* that as it may
(or, maybe, *not)* it
behoves us, before
proceeding further,
to realize that *had*
the body been *stolen*
(as the High Priests would
have had us believe),
then the grave clothes
would have gone missing
too. (What thief would
have risked detection as,
for no good reason,
he spent precious time
removing them from the
body, and stowing
them away? – yes,
and even neatly
folding them!)

Let's face it – we shall
never know, *precisely,*
what that disciple saw,
and what it meant to him,
as he braced himself
and entered the tomb:
what we *are* told
is that when he *saw* it,
he "believed!" – yes! –
just like that!

And it changed
the course of history.

So, what *was* it
he believed? Truth is,
he could find no words to
describe the experience of
stepping out of time and
into the timelessness
of Eternity, where
resurrections take place –
succumbing to
the awesomeness that
filled that cavernous,
and seemingly
empty space.
No – confusion, and
incoherence, were
the order of the day,
with no attempt to
hide them away.

Thus, the story of
the two who had walked
for several miles in the
company of the one
said to have risen
from the dead, but whom
they, too, had *failed to
recognize* – that is
(they said) until he
'broke bread' with them,
a detail of such subtlety
as to reverberate
with truth; yet,
countless the numbers of
those who, down the ages,
have dismissed the story
as merely an attempt
to add the flavour of
authenticity to a
tale that today would be
dubbed mere 'spin'.

That folk as humble
as they, could think to
adorn with such false
subtleties their endeavours
to deceive, is harder –
yes, *harder* to believe
than the truth of what
they had given so
halting an account.

And let's not *burke* the issue.
As well, we have to believe that,
though (supposedly) *concocted,*
the story had, in fact, convinced
those deemed to have been
its very *perpetrators:*
a classic case of self-
deception, if ever
there were one — yet,
empowering them
to emerge from
behind locked doors,
to face a hostile world;
and crucifixion,
for some.

Even in the realm of
science, the simpler of
two *possible* solutions
is deemed to be the better.
So — by that selfsame
token — did not the
faltering account of
what they had seen,
with their response to it
(*and,* yes, those
artless addenda),
have the greater claim
to Truth?

Ode to the Amateur Astronomer

How strange
this human life of ours! –
for some, sleeplessness
a simple choice, an
"Open Sesame" to the
depths of outer space,
but, for others, the
unsought consequence
of their efforts to explore
that inner space, which is
the quintessential Self;
photons – completing a
multimillion-year journey –
the fleet-footed messengers
from outer space;
post-synaptic neurons –
firing simultaneously
in their multimillions –
the massed messengers
of inner truth.

How fearfully
and wonderfully
made, we are! –
how wonder-full,
the infinitudes
of outer,
and inner
Space!

Of "Hyper", Critical

I went on an outing –
no, not to the sea,
but to a *Hyper*market,
where I spent abundantly:

    four paper rolls for kitchen use,
    six toilet rolls – and, *quilted*, too! –
    and tablets, *dozens* of them, to
    meet dishwasher's need;

there's bread flour and tomatoes,
and spring onions galore;
of thick bleach, a litre, and
tablets (yes, yet more!) – but
this time for the toilet, lest
limescale should prevail.

    Of soya milk, three litres;
    organic? Yes, of course –
    and unmodified genetically,
    which I'm sure you will endorse.
    A kilogram of carrots, five hundred
    grams of cheese, oh! – and many
    ready meals, which I merely have to
    freeze: it's all so *convenient:*
    I hardly do a thing: just pop one
    in the oven till the timer gives a ring.

    And – *shame* on me! – I nearly
    failed to mention two *litres*
    of "Comfort": and, of *comfort,*
    that's a *lot...*

So –
for the future that's
foreseeable, I've everything
I need – a statement on which
I'm *sure* we're all agreed.

    But, *wait!* – did I say
    everything?

    I wonder.

Paradox

Friends – dear
beyond words,
and from near
Earth's other end, –
have been, and
gone again, in a
mere four days.
And all too well
do I know now
what it means
not to know
what to do
with oneself.

So –
just as soon as the
taxi had whisked them
round the corner and
out of sight – I went
and lay on my bed,
a rare 'out' for me.
And, rarer still, I
fell asleep: what more
was there to do?

But when I woke –
true – it was
to find that
where they had been,
there was still
the sense of
empty space,
but, as well,
a sense of
added
presence.

.

—— Parcels, and People ——

Parcels,
like people,
come in all shapes and
sizes, and – as with people,
so with parcels – it can,
at times, be difficult
to uncover what the
outside wrappings
are hiding.
But, take heart! –
the wrappings themselves
can be so revealing.

Thus was it
with a parcel
brought to my door
by a plainly-puzzled
postman: to describe
it as unshapely
an unwarranted
compliment.

As long as your leg,
and with a bulge here,
and a hollow there,
it could well have been
a gun, but who
would choose a gun,
to celebrate
my birthday?

It was just then that
the wrappings themselves
began to speak –
first of the care, and
then of the love that
had made it possible
for the sender even to
contemplate the task:
each awkward fold
held down by
parcel tape, each
bulge the object of
affectionate
attention.

Reluctantly
(I had no choice),
I ripped apart
love's labours –
only to reveal
an inner parcel,
gift-wrapped with
still more love.

What mattered it
now: the object
the gift wrap
still concealed?
It could have been
anything, or
nothing at all;
for was not the
only gift that
really mattered
embodied in
the wrappings?

Quartet

Lights lower, expectations rise. The round
of chatter yields to sudden silence now,
as we await the four to take their bow –
from horse-hair, twisted gut, coax 'cilia's sound.

In Indian file they come, our whispers drowned
by rapturous applause. They perch, and peer
at scores, as though for first time seen; we clear
our throats of threatening coughs, and wait, spellbound.

But whetted appetites must further bide
their time ere music's feast is spread, while strings –
to speak with heaven's voice – are tested, tried,
in unisons and fifths (oh, bliss! - that brings
such promise from discord); then, bows applied,
the leader's nod – and beat of angels' wings!

Question Mark

"Making Easter easy,"
is what the advert
promised – backed up by
mouth-watering images
of seasonal delights.

'So', I found myself asking,
'does that mean that people
now think Good Friday was
just a piece of cake?'

Reincarnation

Not quite
mouldy, but
old enough
to have seen
better days:

the fruits of
many trials
(and errors,
on the way) –
the remains of
my brain-child,
my much-loved
multi-grain
loaf.

But,
no land-fill site
for its soft centre
and erstwhile
crispy crust,
in fragments now,
and on their way
to their last
resting-place:
my lawn –

to become,
in their next life,
a blackbird's song.

---------- Second Thoughts---------

'Tic, toc,'
said the kitchen
clock, high on the
wall, near the ceiling,
talking to itself,
and unaware
that it was being
overheard;

irritating, and,
at times, nigh on
exasperating –
that it should insist,
so obtrusively,
on marking the
inexorable
passage of
time.

But –
no longer so.
Rather does it
seem to say that
seconds (sixty to the
minute, and all but
four thousand in the
hour, a hundred
thousand every day,
and millions – full thirty –
in a year) though, in
Man's measure, brief, are yet,
in God's measure, far from
fleeting: each and every one
a Present Moment,
an Eternal Now.

Sikri

I went away
to stay with a cat –
at least, at times,
it *felt* like that.

Young, and friendly
to a fault, she nudged
and nuzzled her way
to my heart; three years
old, I was told, and
"tortoiseshell" her markings:
black and yellow, the colours
of Big Brother; I should have
taken more note
of that.

About the house,
she was the essence of
playfulness: one moment
on top of a cupboard,
crouching, just below the
ceiling, and punching the air
with sharp jabs of her paw,
like a boxer's sparring
partner; the next moment on
the floor, wrapping herself
in a rug.

Sikri her name, but
Jekyll and Hyde
her nature: yes,
about the house, the
personification
of playfulness;
but beyond its walls,
past master in the
art of catching birds.

Live or dead, and
blood-besmirched,
she would bring them
into the house,
to demonstrate to
the world at large
that though the leopard
couldn't change its spots,
Sikri certainly could –
'And take due note of it,'
she seemed to add,
with sadistic
satisfaction.

How could I
do otherwise? –
to ponder afresh,
upon Nature 'red
in tooth and claw',
symbolized by that
sometimes friendly,
but sometimes
deadly
paw.

Special Offer

'My peace
I give unto you,'
he said. 'Not as the
world giveth,
give I unto you.'

But meaning
just what? –
'no greek gift this,
and terms and
conditions
conspicuous
by their absence'?

Or is his peace
that which comes,
not with sheltering
from the storm, but
in weathering it? –
to find, at its
very heart,
not merely
his peace, but
his serenity.

------------ **The Challenge of Christmas** ------------

Though I
gather knowledge
how, when and
where I will,
yet, be it
but for head
not heart – stashed
away for an
intellectual
rainy day –
then would
such time
the better
have been spent
deep-mining
head's knowledge
for heart's
treasure.

But – Christmas
is different: as a
story of long ago,
our knowledge of it
seeming all there *is*
to know. So – we click
on 'File', then 'Save As'
"History, Past and Over",
thereby, as it were
committing it to
memory's cold-store,
lest it take root in
heart's warm core,
to ripen there, in
life-transforming
measure.

------------The Choice -----------

Meaningful, or meaningless? −
the stark choice posed by a
Universe of countless galaxies,
each comprising a myriad
of stars rivalling our sun, and
occupying an infinitude
of Space.

Even the cosmologists
had their problems,
the very notion
bordering on anathema:
that time began with a
Big Bang, when, at a
singular point, and in
an instant, energy −
enough to father
such unimaginable
quantities of matter −
appeared as if from
nowhere.

But specious mathematical
alternatives were overtaken
by hard facts, the Big Bang
the largest intellectual pill
that Homo Sapiens has
ever had to swallow.

The scientist,
within the constraints
of a remit self-imposed,
strives merely to answer
'How?' − the theologian
the more daunting 'Why?',
taunted, as he does so,
by the materialist,
asserting, with seeming
satisfaction, that the
Big Bang, together with
the Universe it spawned −
to say nothing of the
joy and pain, born of love,
and deep-engraved on
any human face −
add up, one and all, to a
mere "tale told by an idiot,
full of sound and fury,
signifying nothing": the
inevitable conclusion
to which we tacitly subscribe,
when we abandon the quest
for meaning in the
miracle
we call
Life.

------------ **The Christmas Present** ------------

No – it *wasn't*
the latest in
I.T. gadgets,
sporting millions of
transistors, etched
into a silicon chip
untouched by hand,
and made, no doubt,
in China...

It was, in fact,
'Just a pair of socks',
as some would say,
'made' (they might well
have added), 'Heaven
knows where!'

Yes! That's *right!*
Heaven *does* know
where – *and* how:
unlike the micro-chip –
the sterile product of
a mass-production line –
the socks the work of
a pair of human hands,
each stitch motivated
by a growing anticipation
of the pleasure it (and
the ten thousand
others it had joined)
would bring to the
recipient, all
unaware.

I looked,
and wondered at
the throw-away
display of skills,
where blue changes
imperceptibly to
grey and back
again; and rounds of
stitches – no longer
foot-embracing –
wheel, like marching
soldiers, to embrace,
instead, the heel:
to me, sheer magic,
but, seemingly,
so casually
performed.

And all this for a
mere Grandad-in-law –
though I was feeling
more like a full-blown
Dad as I slipped them on:
socks that fitted me like
a *glove!*

And – when I'm
wearing them –
I can feel the
warmth of
knitted-in
love.

------------ "The Wind Bloweth Where It Listeth" ------------

Of an age
when the wind –
suddenly gusting –
could have me over,
I was hove to,
sails furled,
and clinging
to a wall,
hoping that
someone, with
the strength (and
an arm) to spare,
would come by
and walk me
the short distance
back to the safety of
house and home.

But – as so often
in life – help came from
an unexpected quarter:
not a pedestrian,
but a passing
motorist; and – yes! –
a *woman* driver!
(How many *men*
had passed me by:
'Someone's bound
to see him, who's
got more time
than I'.)

She stopped her car,
and had to cross
a busy road to
reach me.
'Can I help?'
she asked,
so simply.

I told her of my
plight, and, with
no more ado,
she went back
and locked her car.
'Come on!' she said,
'I'll walk you home:
I live quite near
to you.'

Most would have
dismissed it as
coincidence;
Jung, with greater
insight, would have
deemed it to be
a first-class case of
'synchronicity'.

But, be that
as it may:
Sue, who rescued
me, her brother
Don, and his friend
Tricia, regularly
meet with me now
in ever-deepening
friendship – to
celebrate that
sometimes,
'God moves in a
mysterious way,
His wonders to
perform.'

For wonder it is –
that a gust of wind
on a blustery day
should have brought
all four of us
together,
so.

Till Death Us Do Part?

I looked into her eyes:
the one I loved so much
still there – behind them –
looking out at me.

  Then,
  but a moment
  later, and it was
  no longer so –
  that look of
  recognition
  now not even
  as much as a
  vacant stare:

in an instant,
immeasurable
as time, she had
left her body –
the countless atoms
that had composed it
unchanged: as ever,
in their lifeless state.

  Even so,
  could it not
  be said that,
  having no life
  of their own,
  they had yet –
  in a sense –
  died with her?

And,
I too –
who had yet,
in body,
lived on?

Time Will Tell, Once More –
But When?

It's true: I'm
no longer able
to tell the time –
even though
the sun shines
full on me.

You see –
sundial though I
am – my gnomon
can no longer
cast that
all-important,
time-telling,
shadow
on my face:
with all but its
tip buried deep
in snow, it looks
more like the only
decoration
on a well-iced
Christmas cake.

Oh – snow!
Please go!
I'm *dying* to
tell the time
again.

Transmutation

I took my loneliness
to God, looking for
consolation. But He
handed it back, saying,
as He did so, 'It's a
job to be done.' And the
loneliness vanished, as
I got on with the job
of being on my own –

with Him.

Unwilling Host

Sometimes, we
catch a glimpse
of Truth – as brief
as the sight of a car
flashing by;

    but, unlike the car,
    we know, full well,
    that it's not the last
    we'll see of it –
    however much
    we may wish it'd gone
    some other way.

Best to invite it in,
I think, and hear
what it's got to say.

This poem was written, following a news item during the Iraqi war.

War Games

The other night,
as I lay tucked up
in bed, a soldier was
urinating on a
prisoner in his charge,
the prisoner's offence
no heinous act of
savagery: just theft,
in desperation – the
by-product
of war.

By the time I was
having my breakfast,
they'd had even greater
fun, kicking in his teeth,
then loading him onto
a lorry. And whilst
I was having my
mid-morning snack,
they'd dumped him off
the back, not knowing
if he was alive or dead:
when all's said and done –
what matter?

Afternoon tea in the
garden with a friend –
and yet other members of
the forces of liberation
had dreamed up
a brand-new way of
passing the time of day:
stripping a prisoner bare,
and attaching wires to –
well, you know where
(they'd threatened him
with electrocution
if he fell off the box
they'd stood him on).

I was ending
an enjoyable day with a
tasty evening meal, whilst,
unbeknown to me,
a woman soldier was
enjoying her own little
game, of offering up
an imaginary gun to
another prisoner's –
yes – you-know-what;
when all's said and done,
it was *such good fun!* –
and a welcome change
from bumping off one's
fellow human beings.

Incensed?
Who wouldn't be? –
but the real offender
war itself, whose
innate brutality
can change decent
human beings into
near-animals.

And worse.

What Price A Human Life?

It depends – it would seem –
on where you are, and
what you are doing.

So –
let's start with
Afghanistan. There it
matters not whether
you're American,
British, or even
a member of
the Taliban:
fact is, the price of
a human life is
the mere cost of
a rifle bullet.

But, now *think big* –
think font 72,
and **"bold"**, *italics*
and "CAPITALS":
think ***CHILE!***
There – on the
Thirteenth and
Fourteenth of
October, in the
year Two Thousand
and Ten – thirty-three
men, trapped in a
mine for sixty-nine
days and nights,
were rescued –
the sky no limit to
the money spent.

The world –
breath-held –
looked on,
as so-called
'ordinary' men,
attained their
extra-ordinary
goal of saving
thirty-three souls
from a living death
in the San José mine,
all but half a mile
below the Atacama
desert, in the
uplands of
Chile.

But, as well – yet
unbeknown to them –
they had saved
the soul of
Humanity itself:
at risk of being
shot to pieces, in
the poppy fields of
Afghanistan.

(15.10.10)

62

When the Little Bird Sings -

it's a wake-up call
for me:

hatched in a
South American
jungle, his home
(to all intents
and purposes),
now beside
my bed.

Press One, and he
undertakes to
sing again, just
ten minutes later.

But,
press Two, and he
lapses into a
stony silence,
his task discharged
for another day
(which, as his
silence implies,
is up to me
to fill).

I take the point,
and rise then – to
meet, greet, and
embark on a
whole new day:
God's latest gift
to me.

Words Concealed -
But Truth Revealed

I have it
on Google's
authority
(and, "'What better?",
did I hear you say?)
that the Oxford
Junior Dictionary
has dropped
such words
as 'monk', 'nun',
'pew', 'pulpit',
'saint', 'sinner',
and the like,
to make way for
words such as
'celebrity'.

What's that you say? –
"You're not surprised"?

Nor I.
When all's said
and done, it's
the Celebrity
we worship now,
not God.

Writing a Poem

is like getting married:
you have little time
for anything else
other than your
new-wed spouse;

and sometimes
you have to learn
the hard way, that
she has a life of
her own - for which
she needs space
in which to
live and breathe.

So,
let her be,
right now –

that poem,
too.

RETROSPECT

This long, narrative poem was written in 1989, about eight months after my wife Mary had died, and recalls our life together, and life as it was for both of us, in the last twenty years of her life. It is informal, and, indeed colloquial in style, and was written in the hope of capturing the finer details of the lives of both the carer, and the cared for, and is dedicated to the countless couples who have shared, or are sharing, similar life experiences.

It was not simply
that I lost my wife
but – as I had come
to know it –
my own life,
as well.

It was twice twelve hours
around the clock,
day upon day,
week in, week out,
month after month,
and year on year:

your pillow first –
the L-shaped one –
to prop you up
for breakfast; then,
'A nice warm flannel
for your face.
That's better, is it not?' –
"The Guardian" whilst you wait.
(How avidly
you read the news!).

The breakfast tray lay ready
on the kitchen stool,
your pills set out
the night before:
two Neo-naclex K,
one each, Propranolol, Hydralazine;
remaining quota for the day
stowed
in a separate pot
(lest I miscounted,
or forgot).

Sometimes, I did just that:
come bedtime,
and a tell-tale pair
of bright pink pills
remained,
which you, as like as not,
assured me you had had
at supper-time.
But – fail safe, the system:
so, at my behest,
(but protesting!)
you would take the rest.

With breakfast done,
came dressing time.
How patiently
you suffered day by day
my fierce fights with
rebellious clothes,
my protests at the
crass stupidity
of women's tights!
We managed, though;
and sometimes even matched
the right belt to
the dress!

The first fraught journey
of the day
was through the hall,
the sitting-room
our goal, doors
the worst of all the hazards –
persuaded, as you were,
their width was
quite inadequate
for you plus walking frame.
I teased you –
how I teased you! –
suggesting that you wore
some form of cat's whiskers
which might, perchance,
convince you
that there *was* room
after all.
But, you didn't see
the funny side of that –
nor I, in fact –
and the joke
began to pall.

You settled for the morning
in you favourite armchair –
'Do you want the paper still,
or your tome on Gorbachev?'
(What joy it was
that you could still read
your fill!)
'I'll need to go
to the shops, you know.
Shall I take you to the loo? –
or will you do?
And don't forget
the memory phone:
Number One is Wendy,
Number Five is Joan –
but I'm quite sure
you'll be alright.

Be very, very careful
should you need
to leave your chair;
just remember! –
I'll not be there
to scrape you off the floor
or wall,
if you should fall.
As if you would!
Goodbye,
God bless!
Take care.'
(Strangely,
you seemed to tolerate
the blacker jokes.)

Invariably, the shopping
would take longer
than I'd planned;
and I would fidget –
ring you up,
and you would answer
with that nonchalant 'Hullo'.
'Are you alright?' –
I'd anxiously enquire.
'Of course I am!
Why should I not be?'
you would say,
and so dismiss
the whole gamut
of my anxiety.

Lunch was always
a simple feast:
cottage cheese
with lettuce and tomato,
and, of course,
one bright pink pill,
this time Hydralazine.
"Afters", then –
occasion for one of
my surprises.
So, sometimes,
in lugubrious voice, I'd say,
'There's not much for today -
it's just plain yoghurt,
I'm afraid –
though I do know
it's usually something nice.'
And then,
out from behind my back
there would appear
a Gooseberry Fool, your
Flavour of the Year!

Afternoons
were relatively
unruffled times;
a two-hour rest
ordained long since
for you – so, time when
I could freely choose
what I would do.

A rest, myself?
Not likely!
A walk?
Maybe. Drive into
the countryside to paint?
Perhaps.
Or play my cello? –
No! That's for evening time:
I'll settle for the walk.

Come four o'clock,
and, 'Show a leg! – let's have
a cup of tea, and cake.'
(Oh – yes! I'd learned to cook
as well.)
'There's something nice!'
(I'd made your favourite –
date and oaten slice.)
Thus did we, in our
innocent indulgence,
learn to blunt
the sharp end
of disability.

Evenings were different,
especially so, of late:
not, alas, as they should be –
a time of letting go;
neither surviving
as we used to do,
the hassle of the day.

Increasingly, you wanted
the meal brought on a tray,
the dining-room now
a day's march (it seemed) away.
And TV hadn't, still, the power
it used to have, to entertain:
no longer did we settle
to our favourite evening slot –
you'd try to read your book instead,
then give me such a plaintive look,
and murmur,
'What shall I do now? –
or shall I go to bed?'

'It's only half-past eight,' I'd say,
and vehemently protest
that it was *far* from being late –
(dreading the thought
of ending the day alone –
and fraught).

But, you were insistent,
and I would give way,
and initiate
the long routine
of washing
and undressing time –
and bed.

'Goodnight! and stay tucked up.
God bless!
Don't hesitate to call me
if I'm needed –
my love,
and tender loving care,
are, as you know,
ever and always
there for you.'

Would that I had known
what now I know:
that –
for you –
time itself
was running low.
Oh, God!
Would that I had known.

It happened on Friday,
the Twenty-fourth of June,
and, relatively speaking,
life had of late
been kind to us.
It's true, you were in hospital –
you'd been there for a week –
but just for me to have a break,
and for you to have
some things attended to
for comfort's sake:
a toe-nail that was hurting,
and your gums were very sore;
your calliper had rubbed your leg,
and made it almost raw.

I painted you a picture,
during those first three days –
of the bridge at Freshford,
and "The Inn".

As ever,
you were full of praise.
And, the next two days I painted
the weir at Avoncliffe, and
would have brought that to you, too –
on the Friday afternoon.

But when I came,
as usual,
soon after breakfast-time,
and sought you in the day-room
in your favourite chair and place,
I found you, yes, I found you,
oh! yes, I found you there,
but no-one –
but *no*-one –
had found you'd lost your speech.

My poor, belovéd
Mary dear,
they told me that the nurse
who'd got you up that day
was new – would not have known
that you could speak,
the day before...
God! the horror of it all –
even to me you looked the same,
as I came up to your chair,
but when I asked, 'How's you today?'
all you could do was sit and stare –
gesticulate at me,
and murmur
incoherently.

To think that
all in ignorance
they'd got you up
and dressed you,
put you in your wheelchair, too,
and pushed you
to the sitting-room
to wait for me to come,
and all that time,
my poor dear love,
you'd failed to make them understand
that you had had
yet one more stroke.

It seems that life
was never meant to be
on an easy instalment plan,
for you and me.
Time and again,
the anticipated joy
would explode
into catastrophe:

no use to say,
'Do you remember
that June day
in Nineteen Sixty Eight?' –
you spent it,
unconscious,
on the landing floor
outside our bedroom door.

I had left you
at the gateway,
seemingly so fit,
and,
on a blue-bright
cloudless morning
how was I to tell
that it was not just to me,
but to an era,
that you had waved
farewell?

That day,
speeding workwards,
I had penned some lines
for you –
a blue-bright
cloudless vision
of our future –
even (as now),
I desperately endeavour
to re-create
our past.

All day, by telephone,
I sought,
in vain,
to share those lines with you:
how was I to know
that you were hovering,
day long,
on brink of death –
alone?

When I reached home
that evening, the milk
was on the step,
the door unlocked;
inside the house a stillness –
the antithesis of peace.
I searched the ground floor,
room by room,
and two, three at a time,
mounted the stairs –
to find you,
where you had lain
all day.

My hands still
clutched my vision
inscribed, "To Mary Mine",
and dated
"Seventeenth of June":
".... what does it matter,
but that I love thee,
meet with thee now –
my being with yours,
finding each other
anew,
after the long day's heat,
as early evening's
cool refreshment
renews
the morning's promise,
and we,
at last,
are free
to love
in an eternity
of time,
deprived, once for all,
of the tyranny
of its passing?"

Oh, yes –
no tyranny was left
in time that came to
a sudden halt,
as I pillowed
your unconscious head,
and washed the vomit
from your face.

And four strokes on,
and twenty years
(and, yes, plus just one week),
for us
time ended,
altogether.

Yet have I thought,
these few months
since your passing:
did it not take
those twenty years –
(plus that one week)
finally to deprive time
of its tyranny;
and for us
to discover
that our love
belonged,
not in time,
but in eternity?